Does It Count as Being Homesick If You Are the Only Thing I Miss

Dan Heise

Does it Count as Being Homesick if You Are the Only Thing I Miss

Copyright © Dan Heise, 2023

All rights reserved.

ISBN 978-1-949127-30-0

First Edition

Cover art by Elena Thomas, **art.elenadthomas.com**

Published by Deep Overstock, Portland, OR.

deepoverstock.com

To my family and my friends, near and far.

Act I: Soulmate	1
Does it mean anything when a girl wears my shorts	4
Cycle	8
Persona Non Grata	11
Dionysus	13
Amethyst	16
The Neck Up	19
Act II: Montana	22
Outside Turner Hall	26
Storm	27
Ruin the Flow	28
Ramshackle Glory	30
Kiss or Kill Distance	33
Adult	42
Act III: Illinois	45
New Year's Absolution	50
"Have No Fear of Perfection; You'll Never Reach It"	53
Snake Hands	55
Frog Legs	57

Reincarnation	61
Ancestry	63
I Keep Cleaning My Apartment	70
You Can't Spell Distance Without Dan	75
Act IV: Moonrise Kingdom	83

Act I: Soulmate

I have a problem with the concept of soulmates
Because people will grow up in the same small town forever
And date someone in high school
And call them a soulmate
And to me that wasn't a soulmate
That's just a statistical probability
But then I realize that everyone is a statistical improbability
How the odds could line up to produce lineages
That produced those two people
At that exact time
In that exact place
And in love with each other
It is improbable
I realized I wasn't mad at them calling it soulmates
I was mad that they had found each other
Cause how dare they have a soulmate that's so easy to find
When I had to happen upon a singular random question
On a now defunct social media site
Just to find you.
Everything lined up and you seemed perfect to me
But then again I was thirteen
And how dare I make decisions regarding my future at 13
They gave me another five years to decide on a college major and a career
And I still chose theater
(With a minor in Latin)
Sorry I'm getting off on a tangent
You have a habit of making me do that
Cause I don't wanna think about the real issues
Like why I even have to think about this in the first place

What happens when your soulmate doesn't keep talking to you?

What happens when you feel like you have to pry every conversation out of them?
What happens when they marry someone else and they don't even tell you they're engaged?
What happens when you don't talk to them for five years?
What happens when you get over your soulmate?
Is that progress?
Is it giving up?

I didn't talk to you for so long
And I finally convinced myself
That we are not soulmates
And to prove it to myself
I reached back out to you
Cause I needed to make sure I could still be friends with you
Without feeling anything.
But obviously I could live forever
And never learn a goddamn thing
Cause even though I still have to wrest every word and syllable out of you
Sometimes I actually get to hear you talk
And it is such a sweet sound I did not ever get to hear when I was young
I watch your video
And I see your face and I get to finally see and hear you
And how dare I think
I could ever get over the person I consider to be my first true love.

What happens when living nine hundred miles from you
Instead of fifteen hundred feels like progress?
What happens when everything begins to make sense?
And I realize that a girl I've had a crush on for a very long time looks exactly like you.
What happens when you won't leave my mind?

I still dream about you
And I get very emotional.
You've been to Portland before
I know you'll come this way again
Maybe this poem will change when I meet you
Cause I still believe we will meet
And I will shake the hand of your husband
Your statistical probability
No, sorry.
Your soulmate
And I will smile warmly
And I will mean it
When I say how happy I am for you
I will probably cry
Tears of joy, I hope.
And later in my apartment
I am sure I will sit confused
Crying tears of joy at meeting you
And crying tears of frustration at the concept of soulmates
And how I was wrong with mine
And you were right about yours.
But this is a distant future I am hoping will happen
And not happen at the same time.
Those tears of joy will be there
Those tears of frustration will hopefully not.
But right now, in the present,
I am working on getting soulmate out of my vocabulary
Because it is not something I can call you
It is not something I want to call you anymore.
I am getting over you little by little,
My former soulmate.
My not soulmate.
My friend.
I will live forever
And I will force myself to learn.
And I will call you friend in the end.

Does it mean anything when a girl wears my shorts

Sleeping

She's so still next to me

Does it mean anything when a girl wears my shorts

She just crashed here

Nothing more

Nothing less

My bed is big enough for two

Hell my bed is big enough for five

Does it mean anything when a girl wears my shorts

We spent a long time together today

Me talking drunkenly

Her listening patiently

Hearing me yell about my ex-girlfriends to my friend

As he yells about his

Does it mean anything when a girl wears my shorts

I can't drive you home

It's 1:30 in the morning

She's just gonna crash here

But she's in jeans

She just wants something more comfortable

Does it mean anything when a girl wears my shorts

I think I learned more about her by sleeping next to her

Than by talking with her for 4 hours

The way she snores sometimes

The way her limbs jerk at random times

The way she pulls the covers over her head

The way I find it very hard to fall asleep next to her

Does it mean anything when a girl wears my shorts

I know the last girl to wear my shorts to bed

I know what she's doing now

I know who she's with now

And whose bed she's in

Does it mean anything when a girl wears my shorts

I can see her in those shorts

I can see her sleepy eyes now

I can see her arms around me at night

But someone else is here now

Look at the difference a year makes

But look at what happened the last time

Does it mean anything when a girl wears my shorts

Does it?

Cycle

DEATH
Death scares me
So I'm not gonna talk about that too much
Lest I have a panic attack.
But I do sometimes wonder about my impact.
Maybe my body won't live forever
As much as I wish it would.
But maybe I will somehow.
I just wonder how.
Will I live forever in a work of art?
Create something worth remembering?
The memories of my friends being passed down?
The kindness I have tried to spread?
Or is it nothing more than the fact that
As a kid I skinned my knee on the playground
Leaving some blood in the dirt
That is still there
Now a part of the earth.
Am I the earth?
Does blood count as liquid?
Does it get pulled into the air as part of the water cycle?
You know the old song
Evaporation
Condensation
Precipitation
On my mind.
There are always a lot of things on my mind
It's what comes with trying to distract yourself from the fear of death
Or rather
A fear of eternity
It's called apeirophobia and I hate it
In a way that induces panic attacks

So I have to get myself over that
And cycle through all the things in my mind trying to distract myself
I cycle
We cycle
They cycle
Reduce, Reuse Recycle
The rule of three reigns with an iron fist
Always hooked into my brain.
Am I hooked into your brain?
Will you remember me?
Where am I?
Where is my blood now?
In how many places do I exist?
And is it egotistical to want one more?
Immortality feels so selfish
But keep me with you wherever you go
Do not let me die.
I am so scared.
More scared than you will ever know.
How do you even pray about this?
What do you say?
May my memory live on.
May someone talk about me some day.
May my ghost haunt forever.
Heat death of the sun won't stop my fucking ghost.
Better stop before I panic attack.
Cause I gotta be better at learning how to stop my brain
That frantic manic panic
Remember your Rule of Three
Is three too many or not enough these days?
I reap what I sow
But I do not sow on purpose
But I gather the benefits all the same.
Being kind makes me feel better
And life is hard enough
So I just wanna make things easier for everyone.

Good things shouldn't feel like a reward for being nice
But at the same time
I MANIFEST THAT SHIT
I just wanna inspire someone
I just want people to be kind because of me
Maybe that's how I'll live on
In the cycle of human kindness.
In the constant kindness I have tried to spread.
But wait
If that's the case
Who did I learn it from?
I cycle.
You cycle.
We all cycle.
Remember to be kind.
Help me live forever.
I'm absolutely scared to death of-
Well…
Yeah.

Persona Non Grata

I try to be slow to anger
At least towards anyone besides myself
I know my life is finite
And being kind sounds way more appealing to me than any other alternatives
But you have changed that.
I try to be a light to others,
A beacon of goodness that others can flock to
And be comforted
But you have changed the circumstances
You have not extinguished my light
No, I am still a warm glow
But it's the warm glow of a forest fire
That's just over the next hill
The warm glow of lava
Slowly make its way down the slope
I am still a light
But you are turning me destructive
Something savage and visceral
Using all those words I always killed in the back of my throat
A clenched fist at my side as I hold everything in,
Finally swinging
Stab someone in the back hard enough
And you'll reach their heart
I'm not sure if that's medically correct
But it sure as fuck feels like it
I used to think something was wrong with me for so long
Because when people bought me things
I always liked them because of what they were
Which felt selfish
But now I feel as though it were a pre-emptive
Almost protective,

Strike
Cause now when I look at the Lord of the Rings blanket in my apartment
I smile because I love Lord of the Rings
And I do not throw my fist through a wall because you gave it to me
Those posters are still allowed to hang up
Because I am blessed and cursed with confused appreciation
I try not to be petty
But because of you I am learning
I'm not there yet
Because I waited until the day after your birthday to sever the ties of our friendship
I do genuinely feel sorry
That Christianity never fully took for you
Despite the fact all of our friendship happened because of church
I wanna say I saw all this coming
But who ever wants to say that
About a sixteen year friendship ending
I feel like there is more to say
Because how could this poem possibly convey
Everything we've been through
And how broken it is now
I guess I could thank you
For showing me how to truly feel anger
And betrayal
I hate feeling more complete because of this
How dare you make me feel like a more whole human
How fucking dare you make me go through this at 26
They say to forgive someone seventy times seven times
You and I both know that.
But I guess Christianity never took for me either.

Dionysus

You ever want proof that the ancient greeks were on to something?
Find a college theater party.
They had it right with Dionysus,
And he lives in every single theater student.
Ah the revelry!
Ah the merriment!
How the alcohol seems to flow endlessly.
Ancient choruses espousing their chanting refrains up to the sky
Reciting the lines of our new gods,
Beyonce and Lin Manuel Miranda.
Heavy bass and showtunes reverberating through our new temples,
The frat houses and apartments of college towns,
New stone foundations found in the basement where we dance the night away.
And here I am,
Right in the middle of it all,
Finally imbibing after forfeiting myself the pleasure for 21 years.
Dionysus has finally found me.
Crafted me into his prophet.
And he does not let go so easily.
Even still, after almost five years out of school,
He whispers the secrets to a good time into my ear.
He is the true miracle worker.
Turning this socially anxious,
Meek,
Scared,
Depressed,
Husk of a boy
Into the person, nay, the man I sometimes dream of being.
Telling stories,

Commanding a room.
Confident, brazen, flirtatious, funny, outgoing, brave, stupid.
Finally turn my mind off and look at the wonders I can create.
Makes me remember the song I once sang in sixth grade,
"Look at me, ain't I pretty, it's my city, I'm the king of New York"
I am the king of this bar, this group of people
Fill up my cup and watch the magic I weave.
Little bit of whiskey to make me frisky
Dionysus rubs my shoulders and says
"Look at that pretty person at the bar"
"Look at that pretty person across the table"
Dan is the one who looks away and mumbles,
"They're not interested"
But Dionysus turns his head back around and whispers in his ear,
"Of course they are".
A cup of self-esteem to finally give me the confidence I've never had,
To make me belligerent with loving myself.
Dionysus doesn't make me fight
But make fun of me and I won't stay up for three days straight worrying about it.
No, I finally have a mind that holds nothing,
A brain that is slick to the touch,
Soaked in the rum and booze of "one more why not".
Aeschylus this is not,
Euripides this is not,
I'm more interested in the Homer of the Simpsons that said,
"Alcohol is the cause of and solution to all of life's problems"
Rather than the man who wrote the Iliad.
This is not just a poem,
This is a love letter
To the god who made me realize
What my inhibitors were
And how good I feel being free of them.
A head pounding like a fist against a door the next morning
But it is so worth it

Just to see me liberated for one fleeting moment.
God I could never love myself more
Than when I'm on my fourth,
Why would I ever want to give up the thing
That finally made me love myself
Dionysus
Boy do I love this.
Dionysus
Boy do I finally love me.

Amethyst

I'm scared to ask about our family history.
There are skeletons I am scared to find.
But even more frightening to me
Are the skeletons I look for, but don't find.
Because this means they do not hide in my family's shared closet,
They hide in mine.
I want to ask about alcoholism in my family
Because I feel like I shouldn't feel this good with a drink in my hand.
No one has ever mentioned it before
No one ever seems to get drunk or out of hand at family parties.
Which can only mean one thing;
I am the procrastinated final paper of my family tree,
I am the nervous nail biting of my bloodline,
I am the bad habit,
Forged of rum and booze and an overconfidence that I don't need this,
I can quit because I'm not addicted to the substance,
Just to how it makes me feel,
I can stop whenever I want because I don't even do it every night
Just on the weekends when I can get out of control
And let my over anxious brain bolt for the open door that someone has swung wide for it
And finally let it escape.
Shut it all down for three straight nights,
And love myself how I finally want to.
A vicious cycle of low self esteem
And hating myself
And drinking to escape
And actually loving myself
Only to wake up after a bender

Right back to square one,
Shouting at myself for being stupid again.
A conversation with myself,
A never ending back and forth argument,
An intervention held by just me myself and I,
You know you have a problem Dan you should seek help,
I don't have a problem cause I don't do it every single night,
That doesn't matter cause you do it enough to worry about it
Well then I'll just drink to stop worrying
That's not how it works and you know it
It'll work if I just believe it will
This isn't who we are
This can be who we are if we stopped hating ourselves
We don't hate ourselves
Yes we do look around us of course we fucking hate ourselves
We like ourselves just fine
Yeah then why is sober me the only one who gets depressed?
I'm not talking about this again
You started this conversation now you finish it
Ok fine you know alcohol is a damn crutch but you keep going back to it
Yeah cause I finally like myself
Then learn to love yourself without it
Why when I have the path of least resistance down at the bottom of this glass
Cause deep down you know you gotta stop it before it gets out of hand
No don't take this away from me
I'm just saying it's time for a break
I'm sorry but I can't give this up
Why?
Cause Why would I ever want to give up the thing
That finally made me love myself!

My family has seemed to be afflicted by health rather than vices.
A lasting lineage of poor eyesight,
Bad breathing,

And shoddy hearing.
My grandparents smoked but quit because I was born.
I was a finish line.
And now I am a starting line,
The start of a new vice because they all have to start somewhere,
I told myself I wanted to be remembered
And leave a legacy
But I swear to you it was never this one.

The ancient greeks believed that amethyst warded off the effects of alcohol
So I'll hang an amethyst pendant around my neck
And the neck of my offspring
The offspring I'll have with someone who makes me want to love myself
Drunk and sober.
If you see me with a drink know that I do feel guilty,
But I am fighting a demon that I summoned by myself,
I am running a race that I started and I am trying to finish
Before I have to hand a baton off to a next generation.
I am picking up my own empty beer can before it gets kicked down the road.
I am learning control.
Squeeze my fingers around an amethyst
And hope that maybe
The ancient greeks were on to something.

The Neck Up

I dislike my body
Not hate, just dislike
Not in a way where I feel incorrect in it
But in a way where I feel like it's a word I have to spell out
After only hearing it said out loud
All I can do is guess as to how it's supposed to look
And it's not guaranteed to be right
My body is not a temple
It's just my room back home
I decorate it how I want
But I'm not sure who I ever want to see it.
Why does my body embarrass me so?
I have such modern sensibilities
But a Victorian idea of my own body
The less I look
The less it exists
Can't wear glasses in the shower
So I barely even know what my body looks like naked
I'm always itching to put my clothes back on
Someone asked about that once
And I'm still struggling with the answer
Turn the light off in my bathroom
Cause Bloody Mary is not the scariest thing I can see in the mirror
A bit too much tummy
A bit too much hair
A bit too much in general
I tell others that that means there's more of me to love
I guess I meant more of me for them to love
Not more of me for me to love
I'm only interested in the unique things about myself
Like how I can wiggle only one of my ears
Or curl my toes to pick things up

Or make my eyes point different directions
I don't know how I figured any of that out
When I don't have the courage to look at myself nude for more than ten seconds
So much I don't know about myself
Cause ignorance is bliss
I hate how I hurt randomly
I hate getting older
Even when I'm frequently the youngest one
A knee that slides out of place
A shoulder that hurts
Fingers that crack
A jaw that pops
Everything feeling off
But never enough to stop me
Like if I stay busy
The years won't catch me
One day I'll do something for the last time
But I won't even know it
I think I just assume my brain is what's important
I've always loved my mind more
It's what happens when all your girlfriend's dads
Tell you you've got a good head on your shoulders in high school
You tend to not care about the rest
I just inhabit this body
It gets me from A to B
All I've ever needed it for
I've only ever liked myself from the neck up
Hair that I agree with
Eyes that I love
A face that tries to convey kindness
My head is fine
I'm so vain about that
I've never had a problem with selfies
I just don't take them in the mirror
Cause I'm never interested in the rest of it

I don't know whether to work out
Or work on my perception of myself
I'm just trying to get to the point
When people tell me I look good
And maybe I won't have to be wearing a tux
For them to say it.
Get to the point
Where I start believing them

Act II: Montana

There is a billboard near my apartment
Telling me to visit Montana.
If only it knew.
If only it knew that back when I was 14 years old, I would have given anything to visit Montana.
Cause that's where you lived.
And I lived in southern Illinois,
1500 miles away
Because of course I looked up the exact distance.
But can you blame me?
You were the first person I fell in love with.
I read your profile
And you were everything I wanted
We had the same interests
And we talked all the time
And just remembering it now makes me smile.
A warm nostalgia of being young and in love.
But it's difficult to remember now
Not because of a cold blast of reality,
But more because of embarrassment.
I remember the fact I fell in love with you because you liked reading and believed in God whole heartedly
And were cute.
And remembering that is akin to a steel rod being dragged across concrete,
I cringe at the thought of it.
But that's what comes with age, I suppose.
You cringe at your younger self.
But you do not regret.
And I do not regret it.

There is a billboard near my apartment telling me to visit Montana

And I thank God it did not exist when I was 16
Because I would have taken it as a sign to get in my car and visit you
Like I…. offered.
The verbs change when you get older
And I realize I wanted to write "threatened" there instead of offered.
I am tipping my hand now as to how this is going to end.
It does not end the way I want
But I think it ended the way it had to.
With a slow, eventual drifting apart
Because of the insurmountable distance between us
Both literal and metaphorical.
Not so much a cutting off
Like a knife severing quickly
But more the breaking of a rubber band being stretched too far for too long.
Almost five years of silence,
The space between Illinois and Montana just the empty plains of America
Instead of a challenge to be overcome.
A distance that was just a number.

There is a billboard near my apartment telling me to visit Montana
And I can't remember if it went up before or after I started talking to you again.
I'm trying to think if it matters
Because all that matters to me is we're talking,
But the timing does have some significance.
Before means I took it as a sign to talk to you.
And after means it was a sign I was doing the right thing.
I am constantly still looking for divine influence
In everything that has to do with you.
Your love of God has a way of spreading,
I mean look, His name is still being capitalized,

But the true irony is that you are one of the biggest believers I know
And yet you are the person who makes me most ambivalent about Him,
Because on the one hand he put you in my life
But on the other hand he put you in Montana
And how dare it think it is a special enough state to hold you.
And he put you with someone else
And he put five years of silence between us.
I'm sorry.
This sounds like one of those poems
Where a guy just complains about a girl being with someone else
But I promise on God it's not
Because you are happy,
And I am happy,
I just get confused sometimes.
About why I still dream about meeting you,
About why that billboard appeared outside my apartment,
About why I thought it was a good idea to start talking to you,
I look inward and I just hate myself for all of this
Because I realized at the age of 26
I had hit a point
Where I have known you longer than I haven't known you,
Hit a point where you have been in my life for half of it
And I think about time and its unyielding passage and it makes my breath shorten
And I start to panic
And I need a distraction
So let's talk about the billboard near my apartment telling me to visit Montana.

It takes up two whole signs.
And there is a large, beautiful mountain
With a lovely lake in front of it
And it's a gorgeous day.

A pure blue sky without a cloud,
And two people rowing in the lake
And the large letters proclaiming,
"Visit Montana!"
And I am realizing now that God has a twisted sense of humor.
Because I dreamed of you
And I started talking to you
And that billboard appeared
And I realized that I had three hundred dollars worth of Southwest vouchers
And a four day weekend.
But Southwest does not fucking fly to Montana.
And I do not own a car.
I could not see you easily if I wanted to.
I could not see you easily if you wanted me to.
But IF you wanted me to…
I would take the 12.453 repeating days it took to walk there.
Yes, I checked.
It'll take me longer if I visit that mountain
And row on the lake
And look up at the cloudless blue sky
And realize
That maybe there's more to Montana
Than just the fact that it has you.
And I am ready to find out.

Outside Turner Hall

Those hugs lingered longer than they should have
And I'm sorry my hand glided down your shoulder that way
Maybe you felt my heart flutter a bit during our hug
Maybe you noticed I had trouble holding your gaze
Or that I was trying my best to smile as warmly as possible
Or that I kept trying to find any chance to grab your hand and squeeze it
I'm sorry I'm coming in like a whirlwind
Taking your attention and time
But I have missed you
And you have missed me too
I know because you whispered it in my hear during our hug that maybe lasted too long
To me they will never lost long enough

Storm

I feel like a storm
I blow into your life every six months now
And we talk and hang out and laugh
We catch up on our lives
But we also look at each other longer
We smile more
Look for ways to see each other again
Before my winds blow me back west
I try to find ways to just brush up against you
I stare at your hands and mine shake in anticipation
How would they feel inside mine?
I stammer and stumble over my words the longer you hold eye contact
My eyes drift down to your lips and my sentence stops entirely
How would they feel against mine?

But I feel guilty.
What if we did kiss?
What if we did all these things just for me to leave again?
The dark cloud and rain leaving behind supposedly sunny skies
I do not want to drag you into my uncertainty
I do not want you to be confused about what you want because of me
I do not want us both to feel as though we must continue this
I do not want to untether you from here

I will not be the hurricane that unmoors your anchor

Please weather my storm
Eventually I will calm
Maybe it won't even just be the eye this time
And maybe I will even move on

Ruin the Flow

I think I caught you looking at me longingly
Was it friendship? Just glad I'm home?
Or something more?
Maybe it was the wine running through our systems
Messing with our eyes
Making everything just slightly off.
I was hoping you'd stay the longest
But you were the first one to leave
We stood in front of your car outside
And just talked
Which is what often happens when I'm home.
Just catching up on our lives
And giving words of encouragement.
I stared at your lips
You stared at me
My heart fluttered,
Suspended in the air for a brief moment,
Before plummeting directly into my stomach.

Sorry, can I ruin the flow here?
I just want this feeling I get; this feeling like every late night talk we have in front of your car is the one leading up to our first kiss? That whole bullshit? I need that to go away. Because it's really fucking distracting. Because not only am I not supposed to feel this way about you, I'm especially not supposed to feel this strongly about you, and I ESPECIALLY probably shouldn't be writing poems about it that you will never see. Every time I'm home, I hope to see you, so I kinda have to wonder, does it really count as being homesick if you're the only thing that I miss? Seriously, this keeps happening, and I really need it to stop.

But I can't stop staring at your lips.
I can't stop holding you tight during a hug

I can't help trying to get any chance I can to hold your hand.
I can't help bringing you in for a second hug
Just to give you one more chance to kiss me.
I'm scared to say these things to you.
I'm scared to actually kiss you.
I'm scared to mention these feelings.
I'm scared to mess up this good thing we have.
I'm scared to have you disappear from my life just because I couldn't control myself
I am scared to lose our friendship.
I am scared to ruin our flow.

Ramshackle Glory

The plane drifts across the sky
But I have heartstrings that are stretching and snapping inside of me like rubber bands
The farther I go
The more I feel it
The ripping away
Like Velcro
Only more violent
I got on this plane
Heart as heavy as a stone
Heavy enough to make me wonder how we took off
But wait, no, not a stone
Maybe an acorn?
Like a really dense acorn?
Cause I could feel it wanting to grow and spread its roots
And attach itself to the ground here
Wrap itself around my house
Twist its tendrils all around the St. Louis metro area
This is home, after all
(Was home?
Could still be home?)
But no, an acorn is too happy
It still makes me think about a future
And I can't be thinking of that now
(Don't want to be thinking of it?)
I want something more visceral
I think of a fist
A clenched fist inside of my chest
White knuckled, straining with tension
I think of the song
Your heart is a muscle the size of your fist
Cause it's sitting right there in my chest
The fingers wanting to unravel

Just reaching out for a hand to hold and root itself to
And oh god I held your hand last night
Our fingers did not intertwine
Thank god
This would have hurt more
Cause that's what this pulling apart is
It is not rubber bands
It is not Velcro
It is not uprooting
It is nothing more
Than my hand leaving yours
My fingers reaching out to grab onto the us we've decide we could have had
(We still could have?)
If I wasn't sitting on this plane
But my hand finds nothing
Nothing physical
Nothing more than a decision
To let this go
And continue how we have been
Just with new knowledge of what could have been
And a promise of no regrets
A promise I've broken twice in the past 24 hours
But you don't know that yet.
I lean my head back in the seat and close my eyes
The thoughts shoot by like light particles
A racing mind,
Until one stops.
Plants itself.
Looks me in the eye.
Making my brain shoot a message down to my heart
That clenched fist in my chest cavity
It finally has its epiphany
And my heart tightens with the realization
A bundle of knuckles and nerves and blood now rejecting the truth
But knowing it all the same

This feeling is not sadness at leaving
Oh god
This feeling is terror
Cause I actually want to go back home
For good

Kiss or Kill Distance

When I was taking theater classes

A teacher talked of the concept

That I have rarely heard of since

The Kiss or Kill Distance

The idea was that when you stand close enough to someone

I'm talking nose to nose

You have one of two intentions:

To kiss them

Or to kill them

Love.

Or violence.

It's suppose to indicate that only strong emotions

Make you wanna get that physically close to someone

And some days it seems like an over simplification

While other days it seems so true

I start to think about what makes me get close to others

I remember a time when my brother and I got so pissed at each other

I had to wrap my arms around him to restrain him

To keep us from hurting each other too much

But then again

I also remember me greeting him off the plane with a huge hug

Wrapping my arms around him to tell him I missed him

And how happy I was that he was here

I start to realize that maybe distance should be the real focus

Because intense emotions make us change the distance

I feel anger and I want to push away

I feel anger and I want to gather in to forgive

I feel longing and I want to hold them close

I feel longing and I want them to stay where they are

I've severed a friendship and pushed away

Because I didn't want to forgive them

I've severed a friendship and pushed away

Because I didn't trust myself not to love them

Love and hate being just as close as I need them to be

Just as I hold my brother close so he will not hit me

Just as I hold someone close and will not kiss them

Sometimes it's less about the emotions I feel

And more about the restraint I have to show

So as to not ruin a good thing

I will stay obsessed with the concept

But I shift my focus

Because it's not about the kissing

It's not about the killing

It's not about the love

It's not about the violence

In the end it's always the distance

The dread thing that lives in the corner of my eye

No matter what age I am

I am 14 and it lives in Montana

I am 19 and it lies in Columbia

I am 23 and it lives in Alaska

I am 26 and it has set up permanent residence

In the St. Louis metro area

Making itself feel at home

At home

Disguising itself as the what if

And whispering regrets into my ear

It eyes me from halfway across the country

And does nothing but radiate itself

Making me constantly aware of its presence

No, it feasts on the longing it makes me feel

And every time I close the gap

No matter how briefly

It will always come back

Distance

That thing I become so familiar with

That I try to paper over with letters

And shorten with texts and phone calls

And they do the job for a moment

Until the expanse seems to widen again

And I just want to see you again

When I will hold you close

And I will not kiss you

But I will still feel love

Because I do love you

And I can feel that

No matter the distance away

It just gets easier

When I'm a certain distance away:

Nose to nose.

Kiss or kill.

Adult

I'm opening up a word document less than an hour after you left
This is not surprising
These words will not be surprising
I have written more than I could have ever expected.
But in the end it's often about the same thing
It's always the distance
I told you I don't feel like I'm defined by my distance
And you said the words I dreaded hearing
"It defines you to me"
Of course.
It's never about me
I don't define myself by distance
But others do
Am I not just the sum
Of all the people who care about me
Distance is always gonna define me
Because it's at the center of the what ifs
And here you are
Gently reminding me of that.
As I actualize myself into the storm I've always felt like
All your attention and time in front of me
Now or never
Finally locking your gaze and telling you
"We need to allow ourselves to do something stupid every once in a while."
Who knew that's all I needed to say
To finally feel your lips on mine
Pulling away and telling you that you don't know how long I've wanted to do that
But wait, no
You did know.
Cause I am not subtle.

Sitting too close, holding hugs way too long.
Everything I've ever written coming true
But I only wrote about getting to this point
And never what comes next.
When we talk about how we will move on
Seeing what we find close by
Because too much stands between us
But I've obsessed over the distance between us too much
There is no distance now
Only proximity
I am painfully aware of it
Physically there is nothing between us
Holding hands as we walk outside
Finally having that kiss in front of your car
But the words
They're what matter
All my favorite lines are about you
But the themes always the same
And distance is where we always end
A good luck
And see you when you get back
Where maybe all the circumstances will have changed
Because we are adults living our own lives
We decide what that means
What we mean to each other
Defining our relationships
What does being an adult even mean to me?
Means being at a place of my own
A job I halfway like
Paying bills
Building relationships
But what does it mean to us?
We've decided we can kiss now
Because why deny ourselves what we've always wanted?
We're adults and can make that decision
And indulge ourselves
But it also means responsibility

As I tell you I cannot do long distance
And you tell me you do not want to move
So we do the responsible thing
And kiss one more time
And wish each other luck on our journeys
No flow interrupted
Just changed
Parting as friends
Parting as what could have been
Parting as adults
Parting as we should be
Parting as I go back west
And I'm homesick already

Act III: Illinois

People will sometimes get mad at me for saying I'm from the St. Louis area,
Because St. Louis is in Missouri,
And I'm from Illinois.
Despite being only 20 minutes from downtown St. Louis
And less time than that from Missouri itself,
People will get angry that I don't just say Illinois.
It's not like I have a problem with saying Illinois.
I just got tired of saying I live in southern Illinois,
Specifically near St. Louis,
And people being confused because isn't St. Louis in Missouri?
I really just can't win with them.
The main reason I don't just say Illinois though,
Is because people will immediately think of Chicago.
And I'm a five hour drive from Chicago.
Fun fact:
The Chicago metro area accounts for one fifth of the size of Illinois.
Which is large, I know.
But consider this:
That means there's still forty thousand more miles of state to explore!
Do you know how much more state there is to Illinois?

This is going somewhere, I promise.
I just have a lot of feelings about Illinois
Because, unsurprisingly, I have a lot of feelings about where I grew up.
A fifth of the state is a city, the rest of it is corn and college towns and a state capital.
And yet I miss it all the same.
Being homesick is something I've always had to deal with
But what I never counted on is what I would miss out on.

I went home and discovered what could have been
An apartment twice the size at the same cost
A love who said we may have been together had I stayed
My friends and all the adventures we didn't even get a chance to have.
So much potential I never realized
Because it never had a chance to actualize
Until I got out.
And there is still more I will miss,
Whether or not I know I'm missing it yet.

A complicated relationship with your hometown is nothing new,
I listen to pop punk music for a reason.
I just never knew how the actualization would go,
All I knew is I had to leave
If for no one else than for myself.
And now let's get to where we always inevitably go,
Where my mind inevitably wanders:
Montana
It was never an option
But I know I wanted to go west
And I wonder if that's because of you
Knowing you were out west
That is, west of me
Or west of where I was
That must have instilled something in me
Some preference for a direction
A compass rose you never knew you gave to me
Just resting in the vase of my subconscious
Waiting in the water
Wondering when we were gonna be friends again
Not so it could bloom
But so it could remind me of what else lives in my subconscious
What else contributed to my move
And how my decisions feel like my own
But never are.

I've always believed in friendships.
Rejection never hurts for me too much
Or at least, for too long.
Because someone saying they just wanna be friends is not the end of the world,
Cause goddamn, having friends is the best!
And I am loving this friendship once again.
It's like it was always meant to be.
It feels like it used to
Just with less of the bullshit that comes with being teenagers
And more of the emotional stability that comes with being an adult.
This is how it was always supposed to be.
The distance nothing,
Just two people
Who enjoy talking to each other
Who respect each other
Who know each other.
I send you something you like
And you ask how did I know.
How could I not?
I had been preparing for this all my life.
For us to feel this way
I grew up and got rid of those feelings
And now I can see it all clearly in front of me.
This is a friendship I want to see through to the end.
But poetry has a way of intertwining itself with us
Giving more meaning to everything
As you told everyone you were moving.
And suddenly I wonder about irony.
I wonder about balance.
I wonder about the sense of poetic justice.

Poetic justice,
Vice being punished
Virtue being rewarded

Irony usually being involved.
Have I been vicious?
Have I been virtuous?
Or is it nothing more than a sense of balance in the cosmos.
Distance is something that will always define us
But consistency is key
I don't know who decided on that
Though I continue to have an idea
And He still has a sense of humor.
But His sense of humor is rooted in poetic justice.

I moved to Portland
And the planes don't fly to Montana
And I don't own a car.
Poetic justice as a deity's favorite joke.
Irony at its finest,
Or so I thought.

I still have belief in meeting you.
I have to.
Friendships like this don't happen every day.
At least, I would like to think ours is unique.
A distance
A connection
A love
A sundering
A quiet
A silence
A longing
A reconnection
A friendship.
Illinois
Montana
Oregon
Wherever
Put a distance between us and I will come no closer

But put an excuse to see you in front of me and suddenly I wonder about what I left behind at home.
What I didn't even know I was leaving behind.

Fun fact:
There's forty seven more states besides Illinois, Montana, and Oregon
But God doesn't care.
The balance must be maintained.
The distance must be consistent.
His joke must be told.
His comedic timing is immaculate
But his regular timing leaves something to be desired.
Thirteen year old me is smiling broadly.
And twenty-seven year old me does nothing but laugh in resignation.
Because I thought I had seen irony at its finest
And now I realize I am wrong
As it dazzles in front of me
In a way more brilliant than I ever thought possible.
Poetic justice polishing it to a shine,
And I wonder whether this is a punishment
Or a reward
And what I have done to deserve either one.

Do you know how much more state there is to Illinois?
Do you know how little that matters to me now?

Cause you just moved there.
Cause you just moved to Illinois.

New Year's Absolution

This all feels familiar
I shake in the cold outside
It is New Year's Eve
And I've done this before
A déjà vu I did not expect
The memories rush back
Ten or eleven
Walking around in shorts in the other Columbia
My family around me
Admonishing me for not using my brain
What did I think would happen, wearing shorts in 30 degree weather?
I had an excuse
Being young and stupid then
But now I am older
And wiser, some days
And yet, here I am
Shivering in the freezing temperatures
While my friends drink inside
And you cry to me on the phone
Because your boyfriend just broke up with you
What a shitty way for your new year to begin
What a way for my old year to end
You apologize, I think
It is hard to hear you through the tears and the noises outside
You just don't know what else to do
I tell you it is ok
Because there isn't much else I can say from three time zones away
I could never hate you
I made a promise to you
No matter what, I am there for you
What kind of person would I be if abandoned you now

I say what words of comfort I can
I stand in silence
You sob
I look around
An abandoned computer chair in the vacant lot near me
It's never looked so inviting
I take a deep breath
And tell you I'll always be there for you
I try to make you laugh
Recite the tweet,
"You know the old saying, boys will be trash"
I don't think it's working
I look towards the entrance
I ran outside a while ago
Twenty minutes?
Forty? More?
Because there was a voice mail on my phone
Of just your voice sobbing
And that is one noise I refuse to hear if I can
It is warm inside, with drinks being passed around
They'll be wondering where I am
But I am where I have always been
Standing outside
On the phone
Talking to you
Being there for my best friend
After an hour or more I tell you I'm sorry but I have to go
You say you're sorry also
I say,
As I always do,
You have nothing to be sorry about.
I think I whisper I love you
And to talk to me again soon
But my mind is in a haze
I walk inside
I say nothing
I refuse to say anything

I realize my hands are folded
I realize I am praying again
It's been a while since I have prayed
But I am mumbling words to God now
"Please let her be ok
I cannot be there for her right now
Please let her be all right"
My hands unclasp.
I take a deep breath
You are not religious.
I want to be there for you so badly
But I can't
So I have to ask someone else
I hope you can forgive me
I'm sorry that the creator of the universe
I'm sorry that someone you only half believe in
Is the best that I can do right now.
I hope He is enough.

"Have No Fear of Perfection; You'll Never Reach It"

"Seventy degrees is perfect"
I think as I walk along the main streets,
The sun streaming through the trees.
The breeze picks up and sets back down gently,
And the smell of summer hangs heavy in the air.
You would enjoy this weather.

"And the houses are gorgeous,"
I think as I walk along the side streets,
Gazing at the variety of homes.
Each unique and wonderful,
Each offering something else to like about it.
You would love these homes.

"These woods look beautiful,"
I think as I hike along the trail,
The forest around me shading me,
Granting me a brief reprieve from the warmth of the sun.
I put my hands on my knees and feel the hurt in my legs.
You would be exhausted and smiling right next to me.

"And the view here is incredible"
I think as I come upon the overlook
The historic mansion standing tall behind me.
Downtown and the valley spread out toward the horizon,
Making me take a step back in awe.
Your breath would be taken away too.

"The city is lovely,"
I think walking through downtown,
The people milling about around me.
Every avenue alive with activity,

Almost every person enjoying this warm summer day.
You would finally find the city as beautiful as I do.

"And my apartment is really nice,"
I think sitting alone on my couch,
A drink in my hand.
Netflix plays on my TV, our favorite comedian,
And the light and sound fills the room along with my laughter.
You would be drinking and laughing right next to me.

Yes
My apartment is nice
And the city is lovely
And the views are incredible
And the woods look beautiful
And the houses are gorgeous,
And Seventy degrees is perfect,

But perfection means nothing without you here to experience it with me.
It's taken me way too fucking long,
But I finally understand your favorite quote.

I'm beginning to realize I hate this weather.
I think I'm ready for it to rain again.
Sunny days make me miss you too much.

Snake Hands

Laying in wait at my side
Wanting to take your hand
Wouldn't take much
Just a quick reach
Darting over
And I'd be holding your hand
How lovely a thing
My snake hands
Wanting to just make its way over
Sliding smoothly over to your hand
Sitting there unaware
Not knowing my hand is just waiting
Coiled and anxious by my side
It would be so quick
Just shoot over
Before you know what's happening
It's done
Our fingers laced together
Squeeze your hand gently
To tell you I'm here
To show you how much I care
How much I've always cared
But the snake hands won't do anything without confidence
That's all it needs though
It is patient and will simply wait for it to show up
For me to feed it some confidence
And then it will hold your hand
And so it waits
And it waits
And it waits

And it waits
And it waits
And it waits

Frog Legs

How to boil frogs:
Do not place them in boiling water.
They will jump out.
Instead, put them in water, room temperature.
Gradually raise the temperature of the water.
Bring water to a boil.
The frog has now been boiled alive.

This is, unfortunately false.
19th century scientists deemed it true,
But then again
They were putting mercury in the brims of caps then
So maybe take that with a grain of salt.
Contemporary science has said the premise of it is false.
Thermoregulation exists for a reason.
Science wins once again.

But it's an excellent metaphor.
Getting so used to something
That you don't notice it's killing you.
I think about that a lot.

I think about that concept.
Of going til you give out.
Cause sometimes it feels so apt.
I tell myself to take it one day at a time
And I've lost track of how many days I've said that now.
I keep telling myself
Put one foot in front of the other
Move forward.
But I only see myself moving forward
Until I collapse.
My legs giving out

And my brain shutting down
As I wonder how this could have possibly happened.

I'm out of work earlier these days
And I have no reason to go out.
I have more free time than ever.
But I still feel so tired.
Working during a pandemic
Is this strange mix of exhausting and fortunate.
Hooray, I'm still working
But goddamn if every day isn't harder than the last.
We're busier than ever
And I just feel so angry with people all the time.
We don't open til 9:30
We close at 4
The sign is LITERALLY at eye level
How is this a difficult concept??

Was I always this angry?
I play my favorite video games and I'm frustrated
I shouldn't be dying
Maybe if the developer had made a better game I'd be better.
Or, It's just a baseball video game for fuck's sake, Dan
How are you not better at this?
Just hit the goddamn ball
It's not that hard.
Why isn't this fun anymore?
And here I have wasted another night with watching TV,
Instead of reading
(when was the last time you finished a book Dan?)
Or writing
(when was the last time you wrote something besides a poem, Dan?)
Or watching a movie
(gotta build that brand on twitter!)
But no.
Somehow with all these fun productive things in front of me

I choose to play video games I'm frustrated with
And watch youtube videos I've seen a thousand times before
And I go to bed angry
And I wake up angry
Because I have to go to work and deal with dumb people
And come back home and deal with dumb me
Ad infinitum.
(way to finally use your Latin minor, Dan, what the fuck were you thinking?)

I look at the anger
And wonder why it looks so much closer than it used to
Like seeing a tornado barreling towards you
I put my hands on my hips and wonder
"What are we gonna do about that?"
Is there anything I can do?
Is this a product of being shut in with nothing but my thoughts
Or have I always been this angry and frustrated?
Has the boiling point always been much closer to the surface than I pretended?
I always knew I was angry with myself
Perfectionism has a way of doing that
Of making you frustrated for doing anything wrong.
After I told a friend of mine about my low self esteem and not being perfect
She said "I'm not cursed with perfectionism, #blessed"
And I can't remember the last time I was so jealous.
Perfectionism, holding me to higher and higher standards
That I sometimes reach
But do not celebrate
Because of course I should be able to reach them
That's just what I expect
Now it's time to expect more.
And on and on it goes.

How does that song go again? This too shall pass?
How many times have I listened to that song now?

How long have I been quoting it to myself?
How long *have* I been feeling this way?
Is it time for help?

I'm always an advocate for self care for others.
Seeking help is ok.
But I keep thinking this is just something that will pass.
Once quarantine is over I'll be back to feeling more normal,
That is to say,
Just angry at myself and not at everyone else also.
Which should feel like progress
But the more I say it the more I realize it's not.
Which is progress in itself, I suppose.
Realizing this may not be something that just passes.
Realizing that I'm not coping.
Realizing help may be necessary.
Realizing that I am not ok.
Realizing that-
Realizing that…..

Realizing that the water feels warmer than it did before.

Reincarnation

I know deep down what my problem is:
It's no confidence.
I lack it in every aspect of my life.
Dating
Work
Personal relationships
Myself.
A low self esteem
Making me feel nothing about myself.
Trying to be confident in the things I love
Fake it til you feel it
But my acting skills have never been that good.
I'm only confident in repetition.
Memorize lines until I know everyone's.
Talk to my friends like I've done so many times before.
I'm confident in driving my car
Cause I do that over and over
Why can't I have that in my life?
I've done nothing but live it
But I'm still never sure what I'm doing.
I've been driving for less than half my life
And yet I turn the wheel smoothly and easily
Change lanes with efficiency
Something I never feel in my own life
Where I feel like I'm faking it constantly
Why should I have any confidence
When I'm just winging it every day
God, how nice must reincarnation feel
Knowing you've done it all before
That's all I'm looking for.
Let me know this is something I have done before
Lived a life
Fallen in love

Worked hard
Made connections
Built friendships
Had confidence in myself
That's all I'm asking for
And then who knows what I could accomplish?

Unless I'm the first in my line.
I hope I can do better the next time

Ancestry

They say kudzu is the vine that ate the south

Nothing like that in the Midwest

Not that I can see

Just a vast nothing

That swallows itself

How could I do anything but leave?

It wanted to eat me also

It is older than I think

As I drive by what I think is the property

That my first ancestor to come to America bought

Five miles from where I live

A piece of land in the middle of nowhere

An old land

I drive the backroads

The car keeps flashing the warning

"Lane departure"

It is too new for these roads

There are no lanes

Any tractor on these roads has right of way

As it becomes the road

The houses are scattered

Nothing but fields

It's always been nothing fields

Corn and soybeans

Town is only five miles away

But I feel like I am in another place entirely

Elder and misunderstood

I cannot tap into it

I tried once

When I lifted an ancient and decrepit book

A tome if I've ever seen one

My church's first directory

All in German

I see the last names of kids of I went to high school with

But I saw the Heises in there

My great great great great grandfather

A member of the church I was currently going to

I felt the full force of everything I was

Baring down on me

I never say that's the reason for leaving

But it dug its way into my subconscious

My family

In the area since the founding of a church

In the area

Before the Founding of my town

Ancient

Old

The land records gave me a place

And now I've moved to a different place

Where do I feel like I'm tied to

Portland?

Columbia?

Germany?

Give me a planet ticket and a month

And I'll find out where I came from

The hometown

No, I mean

The actual hometown

1400 people living there now

Home is a small town

But the hometown is a village

In the middle of nowhere Germany

I often joke with my friends

"People in Germany in the late 1700s

Had nothing better to do

But name their sons Johann and not be Germany"

My family has a penchant

For living in places before their founding

The past will never be a foreign country

I understand it more and more each day

Draw a straight line

From me to Johann

Johann Heinrich Christian

I wonder if we would have anything to talk about

I'd have to brush up on my German

But we can talk about the impulse to move

To find something better

Me in tears as I find someone

Who finally understands

Just one hundred and fifty years too late

Wie traurig

Aber auch wie wunderbar

Johann Heinrich

Es gibt so viel, was ich dich fragen möchte

So viel möchte ich dir sagen

Aber fur jetzt

Ich hoffe, das reicht

Ich verstehe

Ich werde immer verstehen.

I Keep Cleaning My Apartment

I keep cleaning my apartment
In the hopes that someone will come over
Be it a friend
Or someone to fuck
Or both, you never know how a night's gonna go
I know to expect the first
But always prepare for the latter two just in case
I keep cleaning my apartment
I always told myself that as an adult I wouldn't
Cause I hated cleaning my house when I was younger.
Why, Mom and Dad, would I clean it for other people to come over
When they're the ones who're gonna mess it all up again?
But there's something about age that makes me understand my parents more
And now cleaning is not about making me look good
It's more of a common courtesy
"People are coming over, Dan
At least clean the bathroom up for them
You goddamn animal."
I keep cleaning my apartment
I mean it's only once a week usually
But I'm beginning to notice it's almost always on the weekend
Like I'm really hoping something is gonna happen
I try to lie to myself and say no,
It's cause it's important to keep my place tidy
But I know the truth.
Who's gonna want to sleep on the floor
Or on the air mattress
Or in the bed next to me
When my place is a goddamn mess?
So I keep cleaning my apartment.
I am freer than I have ever been before

A new city with new people
And yet everything has remained the same
An empty bed
And a sigh drawing itself from my lips
As I wipe down the sink
And scrub the counter
And pick up my clothes
And I keep cleaning my apartment.
I haven't kissed anyone since I kissed her a while ago
And we don't talk any more
I'm beginning to think I messed something up
What if she cursed me?
I wouldn't be surprised
I'm not known to be the best with people
I think I just keep trying to blame my lack of love
On anything besides myself
So I wonder if she cursed me
And I keep cleaning my apartment.
Maybe it's the apartment.
It's a small studio
A total bachelor pad
Where frozen meals are the main course
But I swear I can cook if you want me to
I am capable of trying
Just give me a reason to.
I keep cleaning my apartment
And I think about the girls at work that I talk to
And how pretty I think they are
And how my hands tend to shake right after they leave.
My boss asked me why I looked flustered
And I had to admit to him that it was because I had just talked to a pretty girl
Almost an HOUR AGO
And my heart rate still hadn't gone down
I gave a girl my number after cleaning puke off the front sidewalk
And she never called me

But at least she still comes by work
So I didn't totally mess that one up,
I'll just blame that one on the vomit
Cause I really don't wanna think that it's me.
I haven't thrown up in my apartment here at all.
I'm glad.
I hate cleaning that stuff up.
I keep cleaning my apartment
And the music plays loud
I never talk to my neighbors so who's gonna complain,
I try to dance and have a good time with it
Even though I know no one is going to see this
No one will see the effort I put in
I look at my favorite posters and I love them
But I just wish I could talk to someone about them
I think about rearranging my room,
That is to say my studio apartment,
But I'm starting to shrug and say "What's the point"
I have to shake that depressive feeling off
So I keep dancing
And I can't wait for someone new to see my nice clean apartment
When was even the last time I had someone new over?
I keep cleaning my apartment.
I'm stuck between loving my life by myself
Cause no one can get mad at me for staying in every single night
And watching Avatar the Last Airbender for the seventeenth time,
Stuck between that and hating being alone
Cause I just want someone to care about
And also watching Avatar the Last Airbender with someone else is really fun.
I'm just too scared to ever reach out to anyone
I see myself as the author of a future book,
"How to destroy every friendship by falling in love with them,"
By Dan Heise

A book that I don't think even has a page written in it yet
Cause we're all goddamn adults now
But I get stuck in my own mind
And I look at the worst of every situation
I could always use more friends
Why would I wanna ruin a good thing by even bringing it up?
Deep breath,
You're getting ahead of yourself,
This table is a mess,
Keep cleaning your apartment.
I know it's so cliché
but once again let's hear that definition of insanity,
The one that says:
It's doing the same thing over and over and expecting a different result every time.
But I'm cleaning my apartment.
I was told tidying up is good for you?
Decluttering is supposed to help?
How can what people say is insanity also be healthy?
I think about this while vacuuming
And I'm not dancing anymore
Cause it's all blurring together
How many times
I keep cleaning my apartment.
I keep cleaning my apartment.
I keep cleaning my apartment.
It's been two years, and I shouldn't care but I do
I keep cleaning my apartment.
I keep cleaning my apartment.
Tinder didn't help, Bumble isn't helping, nothing is working.
I know I shouldn't care but I do.
I keep cleaning my apartment
I keep cleaning my apartment.
Maybe at some point I'll realize it's me
And not my apartment.
But I keep cleaning my apartment.
I keep cleaning my apartment.

I keep cleaning my apartment.
What's the definition of insanity?
I keep cleaning my apartment.
It's doing the same thing over and over again
I keep cleaning my apartment
And expecting a different result every time.
I keep cleaning my apartment.

You Can't Spell Distance Without Dan

I'm seeing the pictures

My brother and parents out again

Enjoying drinks at a pub

While I'm drinking alone in my apartment again

It seems like they're going out more often

Every other week is a winery or pub

But I guess I shouldn't be as surprised

I'm gone

That's one less mouth to feed

I'm missing all the traditions

Like pizza on Valentine's Day

And the Demolition Derby

I can't even say "our" traditions

I'm not there anymore to enjoy them

Every day being away gets to me more

And never in a way I expected

The most random of memories always flooding back

Hard for me to even list them all

And it's the small things I never thought about

Like the combination gas station/liquor store

Red Roof on the edge of town

Or the overpass outside of town

Which knows more about me than I want to admit

Sodas and tears littering the ground over the highway

How much of me is still back home?

I know I talk about home constantly

I'm trying to get used to it

Trying to find anything in Portland

That resembles the things I miss

And if I can't find it

I'm gonna have to make it myself

It's been almost five years

It's supposed to have gotten easier

But recently my hands started to shake

When I realized I was starting to feel the same again

A feeling of not belonging.

Wondering what I was thinking.

Depressed and anxious.

Wanting to cry and call my parents.

Homesick.

The most scared I've been in years.

How was this happening again?

A month in I understand

But four and a half years?

Portland was supposed to feel like home by now

And yet

All I wanted to do was go home.

Why am I still thinking this way?

By this time…

Well I don't what I expected

But it wasn't a yearning to be home

It wasn't spending my nights

Thinking about what I'm missing.

It wasn't sudden waves of nostalgia

It wasn't crying to friends here

About my friends that aren't here.

Cradling my head and comforting me

As homesickness crashes around me.

How deep does home go for me?

I'm carrying it with me everywhere

Even when I don't realize it

Still reeling from the time

When I showed up on time to a party

And one of the hosts said

"You're from the Midwest aren't you?"

I always thought it was my heart I wore on my sleeve

Has it really been home this entire time?

Surely there's more to my personality right?

I never thought I had an accent

But friends hear it sometimes

They hear the things I don't

See the things I don't

Because I'm living them

Why notice myself.

Though-

I've been mentioning it more and more.

The place

The people

The feelings

The memory.

Constant nostalgia.

No matter where I'm at

Whether it's Columbia or Portland

I'm talking about home

I'm talking about the place I'm not.

Is this who I am?

Just "guy who does nothing but miss home"?

After all,

You can't spell Distance without Dan.

I'm never gonna know how I feel about home

There's always gonna be what could have been

What if I had stayed put?

What if I moved back?

It's always the questions

Nagging at me

Home is where you make it

That's no problem

It's the upkeep no one tells you about

It's so much damn work

Plus the constant questioning

Is this enough?

Do I belong here?

Do I belong anywhere?

And will I ever feel like I do?

As I walk along the waterfront with a friend

We take pictures of the underside of bridges

And laugh about art

And talk about eyesight

I remind myself why I love this city.

When I go home

And drink around a bonfire with friends

And visit my favorite spots

I will be reminded of why I love this town.

I may always be split into two

I may never have a good answer to my questions,

The endless questions I keep asking.

But I'm slowly realizing….

I'm becoming more okay with that

Because I'm learning to enjoy the questions

Enjoying the search for the answers

Enjoying home

Maybe I'll never be content

I'll never know it all

But in the meantime

I have people I love dearly

And there are people who love me

And care about me

Wherever I go.

What more do I need to know?

…

I finally understand it.
It will always count as being homesick
No matter who I miss
Cause I always will
I miss everyone
Everywhere
All the time.
How lucky am I
To know I'll always be homesick

Act IV: Moonrise Kingdom

"You're taller than I thought"
The first words she says to me in person.
I am five foot eight but I feel ten feet tall.
And we side hug
And I run back for my wallet
And we wait awkwardly for our food
And we sit outside
And we talk for three hours.
We talk about Lord of the Rings and Marvel and movies and actors and tv shows and tattoo ideas and relatives and TikTok and books and reading piles and everything in between
Exactly what you would expect.
Her laughter is bright and loud.
She shrieks in delight at some of my tattoo ideas.
Every dog that passes is "baby" in a cooing voice.
And I smile.
Because this is friendship.
And with every passing minute,
I kill all those old words in my head.
All those old ideas.
About Soulmates
About Montana
About Illinois.
I do not need them anymore.
I do not need these ideas.
They only get in the way of what this is:
This is two friends having lunch.
Finally closing the distance that separated us for so long
And being happy in that simplicity.
No more divine intervention than finding a needle in a haystack
No less divine intervention than a lost pet returning home.

At one point I tell her Moonrise Kingdom is one of my favorite movies
And she says "Oh of course"
Like she knows.
And she does.
No need to explain
Why I like the movie about the distance between two people shrinking
Two people just trying to be together
And finding a way to work
The fulfillment that comes
With getting what you've always wanted.
She already knows.
And I smile
Because of course she knows.
How could she not?
Did we not share a similar past?
I am someone who lives with distance
I finally close it and look what I find.
Friendship.
The inevitability of it all.
I called it a cosmic joke.
But it is not.
Because there's no punchline at the end of this.
No, because this is a story being told
And we are finally nearing the end of this arc
These feelings and friendship and distance and breaking apart and reconnection and friendship
I've always wanted to know where it all goes
And now I can't believe I'm here
Fifteen year old me keeps wanting to say
"This is why you love her"
And I shrug and simply say
"This is why we're friends"
And that shuts him up.
I am content to sit in front of her and listen
For hours

The fulfillment of finally getting what you want

Before I leave she says these words:
"Tell me when you get home safe"
And I know she cares.
Of course she does.
A photo to commemorate this
A caption saying
"Meet your internet friends, y'all"
We're already saying this will happen again
We're not saying it with the hope in our voices
Like we did when we were saying those words
When we were fourteen.
No, there is a certainty this time
The certainty that comes with being adults
And knowing that where we are
Is exactly where we're supposed to be
Despite the years
And the distance
And the Montana
And the Oregon
And the Illinois.
Put a distance between us
And I'll care about her all the same.
How beautiful it is to have friendship assumed
And not guessed.

It's all denouement now.
No cliffhanger ending
No bombshell finale.
There is nothing more to say about us.
I hope I never write another word about her.
I already know I will not.
Not because she doesn't deserve them
But because I do not need to anymore.
The old words and feelings gone.
Replaced by the only one that matters now:

Friend.
The final words I want to write about her:
I told you I would call you friend before the end.

        Tell me when you get home safe.

Photo by Elena Thomas.

Dan Heise is an author originally from Columbia, Illinois, near St. Louis. He went to school at Southern Illinois University Carbondale, where he studied theater, specializing in acting and playwriting, while also minoring in Latin.

When he is not writing poems or plays, Dan can be found watching baseball, or hanging around the comedy and improv scenes.

This book was written while he was living in Portland, Oregon. This is his first book.